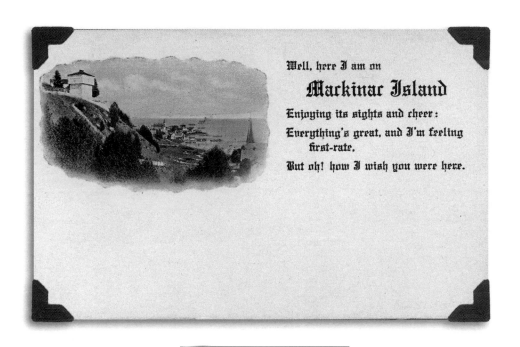

Well, here I am on

Mackinac Island

Enjoying its sights and cheer:

Everything's great, and I'm feeling
    first-rate.

But oh! how I wish you were here.

WISH YOU
WERE HERE

Old Indian Trail, Mackinac Island, Mich.

WISH YOU WERE HERE

AN ALBUM of VINTAGE MACKINAC POSTCARDS

STEVEN C. BRISSON

Mackinac Island, Michigan

Wish You Were Here
An Album of Vintage Mackinac Postcards

by Steven C. Brisson
Curator of Collections
Mackinac State Historic Parks

Design by Group 230, Lansing
Photography by David Woods

Mackinac State Historic Parks
PO Box 370
Mackinac Island, Michigan 49757

Library of Congress Cataloging-in-Publication Data
Brisson, Steven C. (Steven Charles), 1967-
    Wish you were here : an album of vintage Mackinac postcards / Steven
C. Brisson.
        p.cm.
Includes bibliographical reference and index.
    ISBN 0-911872-80-9 -- ISBN 0-911872-79-5 (pbk.)
  1. Mackinac Island (Mich. : Island)--History--20th century--Pictorial
works. 2. Mackinac, Straits of (Mich.)--History--20th
century--Pictorial works. 3. Postcards--Michigan--Mackinac Island
(Island) 4. Mackinac Island (Mich. : Island)--Description and travel.
5. Mackinac, Straits of (Mich.)--Description and travel. I. Michigan.
Mackinac Island State Park Commission. II. Title.
    F572.M16 B77 2002
    977.4'923--dc21
                            2002012634

First Edition
First Printing   3500 copies, soft cover
                      1000 copies, hard cover

Printed in the United States of America

LESLIE AVENUE.   COPR. DETROIT PHOTOGR

Wish you could take a walk with us on
this beautiful island. Ella thinks
it is the prettiest spot she has ever seen.

Mackinac postcard message
August 30, 1909

IF YOU CAN'T COME TO MACKINAC ISLAND
HERE I SEND THE ISLAND TO YOU

ARCH ROCK   OLD MISSION CHURCH   OLD BLOCK HOUSE   SUGAR LOAF ROCK

TABLE OF CONTENTS

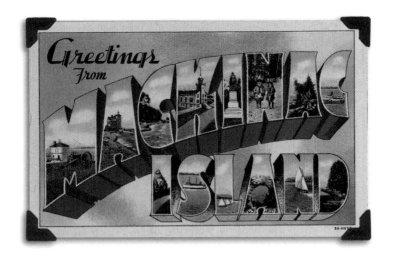

FOREWORD

Istory is sometimes found in unusual places. Mice steal away bits of paper to build nests, buttons drop between floorboards and a trash pit from one era becomes historical evidence for later eras. Travelers to the Straits of Mackinac region do not think of themselves as "making history" when they vacation, but they continue a tradition that is older than European settlement. The Straits of Mackinac region has always been a gathering place, first for Native Americans, then for European settlers, and since the middle of the nineteenth century for recreational travelers. Throughout the twentieth century tourism was the major industry here and postcards the most frequently found and most affordable historical evidence of the pastime.

From vacation albums, from dresser drawers and from the accumulated papers of many homes come stacks of postcards—sometimes written, mailed and received, but often unused mementos. Over the last decade, Mackinac State Historic Parks has deliberately and systematically collected postcards and souvenirs that help tell the story of travel to Mackinac. These picture views not only portray vacation travel; they depict changing times, places, buildings, clothing, transport, attractions and tastes. In these brightly colored images we find a capsule history of Michigan's most popular travel destination.

In this book Mackinac State Historic Parks Curator of Collections Steven C. Brisson has assembled a fascinating assortment of postcard views. Steve has taken the lead in our museums in strengthening twentieth-century collections. He knows them well. The collections that we preserve, the exhibits we present and publications such as this would not be possible without the strong commitment of the Mackinac Island State Park Commission to the preservation of Straits region history. Park Commission Chairman Dennis O. Cawthorne and all of the Commissioners have our sincere appreciation for their ongoing support.

Carl R. Nold
Director, Mackinac State Historic Parks
Mackinac Island State Park Commission

SOUVENIR FOLDER of
MACKINAC ISLAND,
MICH.
GEM OF OUR GREAT
INLAND LAKES.

POSTAGE
ONE
CENT
WITHOUT
MESSAGE

Arch Rock.

M_____

_____

_____

TUEBOR
SI QUAERIS PENINSULAM AMOENAM
CIRCUMSPICE

Published by The Island Art Store

Historical Souvenir
of
MACKINAC
ISLAND
IN COLOR

UNITED STATES
2 CENTS

The Straits Country
MACKINAW CITY,
MACKINAC ISLAND,
ST. IGNACE, MICH.

Old Block House

Copyright 1926 by G. H. Wickman

SOUVENIR
of
MACKINAC
ISLAND MICH.

POSTA
1¼ ¢
WITHO
MESSA

_____

_____

COPYRIGHTED 1935 BY G. H. WICKMAN, MACKINAC ISLAND

INTRODUCTION

THE PICTURE POSTCARD: A BRIEF HISTORY

A little piece of paper with a picture on one side and space for a message, address and postage on the reverse is likely part of every vacation across the globe. Most travelers purchase them either for mailing or to be tucked away with other souvenirs. The postcard seems as if it has been around as long as there have been places to go and friends to receive "wish you were here" greetings. But the picture postcard did not exist until little more than a century ago. It owes its origin to a variety of factors including changes in postal regulations and improvements in cost-effective color printing.[1]

Picture-less postcards, with one side for messages and the other for address and postage, first appeared in the 1860s in Austria and other European countries. Cheaper to produce and mail than letters, the postcard was an inexpensive way to deliver news. The first United States postcard was introduced in 1861 by J. P. Carlton Company of Philadelphia (the copyright soon transferred to H. L. Lipman). These cards were primarily used by advertisers for mass mailings. Companies bought them in quantity and printed either messages or illustrations of products on the back. In 1873 the United States government issued its first postal card with pre-printed postage. From 1873 until 1898 only postal cards issued by the U.S. Post Office could be mailed for the one-cent rate. Privately printed cards could still be sent, but required a two-cent stamp. Like the Carlton/Lipman cards, government issued cards were primarily used by businesses for mass mailings.[2]

The idea of producing cards with souvenir views developed from the advertising postcard and government issued postal cards. World expositions were the venue for the introduction of the picture postcard. Souvenir picture views were produced for the Centennial Exposition in Philadelphia in 1876. Several different sets of "album cards," with blank backs, were issued as souvenirs of the exposition. Though not intended for mailing, some were nonetheless postcard size. A link to later picture postcards is seen in selling printed views as souvenirs, as well as the concern to make the view attractive and use high-quality printing. The Universal Exposition in Paris in 1889 issued one card, sold at the base of the Eiffel Tower (built as part of the exposition). Visitors could buy this printed image of the tower upon entering at the bottom and post it at a government station at the top.

Example of 1898-1907 undivided back postcard. Only the address could appear on this side.

The 1893 World's Columbian Exposition in Chicago introduced picture postcards to the United States. Chicago printer Charles W. Goldsmith issued several sets of official souvenir postcards of the fair. These high-quality lithographs printed on government issued one-cent postals proved an immediate success with the public. Other printers issued unofficial sets. These souvenir issues were the first picture postcards sold in the United States. After 1893 several printers across the country began issuing view cards, usually intended as souvenirs of a city or popular resort. Many of these cards, now referred to by collectors as "pioneer views," carry the words "souvenir." No publishers marketed cards nationally on a large scale. Most produced cards locally for the immediate tourist trade. The postcard collecting hobby began to flourish in Europe, but had not yet come to the United States. A deterrent was that the cards published after the Columbian Exposition and before 1898 had to be printed on government issued postals or carry a two-cent stamp. In 1898 the "Private Mailing Card Act" was passed which allowed privately produced cards to be mailed for one cent. Production and demand for souvenir picture postcards grew rapidly. Until 1901 "Private Mailing Card, Authorized by Act of Congress, May 19, 1898" had to be printed on the address side. As on advertising cards and government postals, only the address could be carried on the stamp side of the card. The view and message

A post-1907 card showing address to the right, message to the left. The image could now fill the entire front side.

had to share the other. Beginning with England in 1902, most major European countries allowed both the address and message on the postage side. United States law was changed in 1907 with the message and address separated by a vertical line (collectors refer to these as "divided backs"). Postcards to this day carry this line, with the address to the right and message to the left.[3]

A postcard and the photo (from the original glass-plate negative) used to create it. Note the ship added in the distance.

The postcard collecting craze sweeping across Europe entered America in the first decade of the twentieth century.[4] Hundreds of thousands of souvenir cards were printed and sold each year. National collecting clubs formed to promote postcard trading. No respectable parlor was now complete without postcards. Stationers seized on the opportunity and produced albums with die-cut pages to hold cards. The types of views available quickly went beyond the shots of towns and popular resorts of the pioneer postcards. Patriotic, religious, comic and particularly holiday greetings became very popular. The U. S. Post Office reported 667,777,798 postcards mailed during the 1908 fiscal year. The number increased to nearly one billion in the next decade, before the collecting craze subsided. A major blow to the popularity of postcards was the introduction of the folded greeting card, which eventually eliminated postcard holiday greetings. Postcards, especially views, remained popular, but became an ordinary part of any vacation.[5]

The development of postcards after the 1907 act focused on changes in printing techniques. Most postcard images originated with a photograph and were produced by a printing technique such as

The printer has cleaned up the streets and removed the bicycle from next to the lamp post.

lithography. At the turn of the century the Germans were the best lithographers in the world. Most cards printed prior to the protective tariff of 1909 came from German firms. Some cards were produced domestically by existing printing companies. Early U. S. producers include E. C. Kropp, V. O. Hammon, The Rotograph Company, Curt Teich, L. L. Cook and Detroit Publishing Company who continued printing cards well into the twentieth century. Each firm's specific printing process was a carefully guarded secret, both in Europe and the United States. Detroit Publishing Company, for example, employed and adapted a Swiss process called "Photostint." The sharpness of the views and color rendering are stunning. Today nobody knows exactly how the process worked. Countless smaller publishers and local photographers also produced cards. Some simply issued postcard sized photos (called "real photo" cards by collectors). Others contracted with German or American printers to produce cards from their images.

With the end of the golden age of postcard collecting in about 1915, the quality of postcards slipped. Companies used cheaper printing processes and introduced white-bordered cards to save ink. The "white border era" lasted until about 1930. From 1930 to 1940 cards with a linen-like texture were most common (the "linen era"). Although the paper quality of these cards is higher, cheap ink was used and the gaudy images are often fuzzy. In 1939 improvements in color photography gave rise to a new process called "photochrome." Postcards could be reproduced from original color images, allowing a more true reproduction of the subject. By the early 1950s chrome cards almost completely replaced earlier techniques and the "chrome" era continues today.[6]

MACKINAC POSTCARDS

Mackinac Island developed into a major Midwestern summer resort after the Civil War and was in its heyday at the turn of the century. Travelers escaping congested cities soaked up the island's natural and historic charm. Many of the tourist shops sold souvenirs as mementos of the trip and the island presented a first-rate opportunity to sell souvenir picture postcards. At least three "pioneer" island views were published by national companies prior to 1898.[7] After the passage of the Private Mailing Card Act production of Mackinac views took off immediately. Mackinac postcards, both in volume and style, followed national trends. All the leading publishers issued numerous Mackinac views. Surviving examples indicate that Detroit Publishing Company, Curt Teich and V. O. Hammon were the largest distributors. Numerous examples also exist from the Kropp, Cook, Rotograph and H. C. Leighton companies.[8]

Island photographers entered the postcard business at an early date. Photo souvenirs had been sold at Mackinac since the dawn of photography in the 1860s. The most common photo souvenir was the stereoview. The stereoview was a double-sided image produced with a special camera, to be seen in three dimensions when viewed through a stereo viewer. Midwest firms and local photographers produced Mackinac stereoview images. In the 1860s and 1870s island merchants John R. Bailey and Fenton & Wendell marketed the majority of these images, produced for them by outside photographers.[9] In the 1880s and 1890s photographers Henry J. Rossiter and Foley Brothers (Edward, Reuben and John) opened studios on the island. Charles G. Agrell operated a shop in St. Ignace from the early 1880s until about 1907. He occasionally also had a shop on Mackinac Island and ran Foley's Gallery in 1885. Rossiter and Foley Brothers produced stereoviews, views on cabinet cards (4 x 5 inch photos mounted to heavy card stock) and also produced individual portrait souvenirs. Surviving Foley images include several of steamship passengers and numerous shots of tourists on Arch Rock. The Foleys apparently set up a camera at the latter location to peddle photos to tourists. They also sold jewelry, agate goods and Indian curios in their shop. John Foley relocated to Petoskey in about 1905, and operated a studio there until 1946.[10]

There are no known Foley postcards of Mackinac Island. At least five photos credited to Rossiter were published as postcards by E. C. Kropp prior to 1907. Whether Rossiter was entering the business or the Kropp company was simply using a local photographer to provide a service is unknown. Although Rossiter appears to have continued operations on the island until sometime between 1912 and 1915, there are no other postcards credited to him.[11]

An 1880s souvenir folder of island scenes. The single page folds out to reveal a dozen highly-detailed engravings. A variety of souvenir booklets and photos, such as stereoviews, catered to the tourist's need for a graphic image to remember Mackinac.

The two most prominent island photographers of the first half of the twentieth century, William H. Gardiner and George Wickman, entered the postcard business in full force. Both sold standard photo views in a variety of formats and offered traditional photo services. The popularity of stereoviews was ending and both Wickman and Gardiner began producing postcards in the early twentieth century.[12] Although Wickman supposedly had exclusive rights for the retailing of Kodak film supplies, Gardiner also dealt in Kodak films and cameras.[13] Both Gardiner and Wickman published souvenir view booklets.

William H. Gardiner
ca. 1900

Gardiner arrived at Mackinac from Detroit in about 1896. Nearly 4,000 of his glass-plate negatives have survived. From his summer studio on Mackinac Island and a winter one in Daytona, Florida, he offered a full line of photographic services, doing both commercial work and portraiture. He also sold regular black and white and hand-colored views, framed or unframed.[14] To make postcards of his images, Gardiner appears to have dealt exclusively with the Detroit Publishing Company. Based on surviving examples, the number of views produced from Gardiner negatives and sold by him appear less than Wickman's. This may be due to the nature of Gardiner's retail business. Gardiner probably garnered more of his business through traditional photographic services than did Wickman. Possibly other unaccredited Gardiner photographs were used for Detroit Publishing Company views, and sold to other retailers. The Gardiner negative collection owned by Mackinac State Historic Parks contains dozens of Foley Brothers' images which he apparently acquired, providing an interesting lineage in the history of photography on the island.

Wickman's guidebook featured images used on his postcards.

Wickman, who arrived at Mackinac a few years after Gardiner, is first noted in the 1899 Michigan Gazetteer. Not much original Wickman material survives. He did not offer a full range of photographic services, but operated a more extensive souvenir business. Wickman was by far the largest retailer of cards on Mackinac Island. Some of the earliest attributable Mackinac views, and the earliest printed by German firms, bear his name. For a time he apparently published these views himself but by the 1910s he was dealing exclusively with Curt Teich in Chicago. From then through the 1940s Wickman was the largest retailer of Curt Teich views on Mackinac Island, as indicated in the company ledgers.[15] It is known that some views were produced from Wickman's photographs by the original negatives that survive from his studio.

A number of Mackinac hotels and souvenir shops such as Shama's, Schwegler's and Edwards' ordered cards from Curt Teich. The name of the business ordering the card is indicated on the back; otherwise the views are identical. Clearly others could order views taken by Wickman. By 1950 Wickman's business was carried on by Robert Benjamin. The earliest Benjamin views were reissues of those from the last years under Wickman. Benjamin remained the largest retailer of Curt Teich views until the publisher went out of business in 1974.[16] In the 1940s island photographer Clarice McKeever had Curt Teich publish a number of her photos as postcards. Like Wickman and Gardiner she sold varied photo souvenirs out of her shop, known as "The Studio."[17]

Mackinac hotels and other store owners ordered cards from German firms and leading U.S. manufacturers. Doud's, for instance, ordered cards from the Albertype Company of Brooklyn, New York, and Shama's dealt with both Curt Teich and E. C. Kropp. Other card producers issued island views with no notation of the retailer. The majority of surviving examples, including ones for Curt Teich and Detroit Publishing Company do not list individual retailers. The postcard salesman likely made contact with every outlet on the island.

Leather, wood, plastic and other materials have all been used to create postcards. This leather pillow postcard (front and back) was stuffed with fragrant balsam needles. Merchant John B. Doud is remembered for selling these on the island, although Gardiner also carried them in his shop.

Postcards are visual documents of twentieth-century Mackinac Island. Yet, except for "real photo" postcards, no postcard is an actual photograph. Though they start out as a photograph, they are a printed item akin to an engraving of a painting. Alterations were often made to enhance the appeal of the card or to simplify an image for coloration or printing purposes. Foliage, people, ships, clouds, etc. were added to images. Sometimes buildings, people and landforms were obliterated by the coloring process. Unwanted elements, such as manure on the street, were removed. Colors on early postcards are not always accurate because this was often left to an artist who had never seen the subject. Sometimes color samples were provided when the color was crucial, but usually it was left to the imagination of the printer.

Here is a sampling of Mackinac postcards from the first half of the twentieth century. Each image captures a moment in time. In most cases, the subjects pictured continue to be favorites for present-day postcards. Some places no longer exist, however, or are places that do not hold the same fascination for today's visitors.

Gardiner sold numerous island scenes as either regular prints or hand-tinted prints such as these.

The creation of a postcard: The process usually began with a black and white photo (top right). The watercolor sketch (right) adds small boats, removes or consolidates features and gives the printer an idea for color choices, cropping and overall look. The original photo is retouched (bottom right) highlighting features and adding a passenger vessel (leaving out the small boats from the sketch). More importantly, Grand Hotel has been increased 50% in size! The final version (above). The company provided instructions advising the designer to "please use best judgement as to colors of buildings, docks etc. and be sure pleasing effect is achieved."

Photos and sketch, Lake County (Illinois) Discovery Museum, Curt Teich Postcard Archives

A NOTE ON PICTORIAL SOUVENIRS

Interspersed through the postcards are images of pictorial souvenirs such as paper weights, spoons and ceramic wares including souvenir plates, porcelain items and stoneware. During the latter nineteenth century these mass-produced objects were introduced in great quantity. Sterling silver souvenir spoons and souvenir plates became popular following the 1876 Centennial Exposition in Philadelphia.

This souvenir postcard captures another favorite Mackinac souvenir, Native American baskets on sale in front of the Fort Garden (now Marquette Park).

Collecting and gathering keepsakes from trips was an age-old custom. Mackinac visitors purchased a variety of birchbark items crafted by the local Ottawa. Along with souvenir view books, stereoviews and postcards, three-dimensional pictorial souvenirs preserved an image of the place visited.

Souvenir pictorial china is a three-dimensional counterpart to the picture postcard. Often, the same images were used on porcelain keepsakes. The heyday of these pieces, largely produced in Germany, was between 1890 and 1930. This is roughly the same time as the postcards reproduced in this book. Most Mackinac shop owners who sold postcards also dealt in other souvenirs. Like postcards, some souvenir pictorial china is stamped on the back with both the manufacturer's mark and the retailer who ordered it. From surviving examples it appears that Wickman was active in the souvenir china trade.

Trinket box, Germany, ca. 1900. Pitcher by Jonroth, Germany for Japan Art Shop, Mackinac Island, ca. 1910.

NOTES

[1]Martin Willoughby, *A History of Postcards*, New Jersey: Wellfleet Press, 1992: 7-10.

[2]Dorothy B. Ryan, *Picture Postcards in the United States*, 1893-1918, New York: Clarkson N. Potter, Inc., 1982: 1-2. J. R. Burdick, ed., *Pioneer Post Cards*, J. R. Burdick, 1957: 6-7

[3]Ibid. 3-14

[4]The Post Office also implemented Rural Free Delivery in 1898. Until that date home delivery was made only in towns of 10,000 or more, then only 25% of the population. People in rural areas had to pick up their mail in town. Hal Morgan and Andreas Brown, *Prairie Fires and Paper Moons*, Boston: David R. Godine, 1981: xiii.

[5]Ibid. 15-32. Robert A. Olmsted, "Vintage Postcards as Historical Images: Ghosts from the Gipper's Era," *Conservation Resource Management*, National Park Service (2000) 23:10: 5-9.

[6]Olmsted

[7]Burdick: 41; Ryan: 13.

[8]Information on postcard producers and numbers is gleaned from the Mackinac State Historic Parks collection. A full statistical breakdown has not been completed.

[9]Bailey's Drug Store offered stereoviews published by several different sources: Jenney & Miller of Flint, J. A. Jenney of Detroit (probably the same firm), Land Brothers of Detroit, Black & Company of Detroit and Whitesides of Marquette. Fenton & Wendell (later Fenton) offered views produced by P. B. Greene and possibly others.

[10]Information on early island photographers provided by David Tinder, 1995.

[11]Michigan State Gazetteers, 1911-1917.

[12]The Gardiner Collection of negatives is part of the Mackinac State Historic Parks historical collection. It contains nearly 4,000 glass plates. A small number of the images are marked "Foley." A number of original Wickman glass plates and film negatives are preserved as part of the MSHP Emerson Dufina collection. This includes a number of stereoview negatives clearly predating Wickman.

[13]Otto W. Lang, "The Reminiscences of Otto W. Lang," 1975 (unpublished oral memoir transcribed by Mackinac Island State Park Commission): 21. Mackinac State Historic Parks.

[14]Lisa Dziabis Calache, "William Henry Gardiner (1861-1935); An Early Canadian/American Photographer," *Photographic Canadiana* (September – October 1998): 8-13.

[15]Curt Teich & Co. Geographic Index, Mackinac Island and Mackinaw City [ca. 1913 – 1975 company records of card sales]. Curt Teich Postcard Archives, Lake County Discovery Museum, Wauconda, Illinois.

[16]Ibid.

[17]Ibid.

Cobalt blue sugar bowl and creamer, ca. 1905.
Porcelain cracker jar with Fort Mackinac scene,
made in England for John W. Davis & Son,
Mackinac Island, ca. 1900.

POST CARD

*Dear Lizzie—I am having my vacation now and spending a week of it
up here on this beautiful island of Mackinac. We have walked miles
and enjoyed every minute so far . . .*

-Miss W. E. Dewar, July 23, 1909

This is where the rich live in the summer.

-Richard, August 26, 1906

EARLY
MACKINAC CARDS

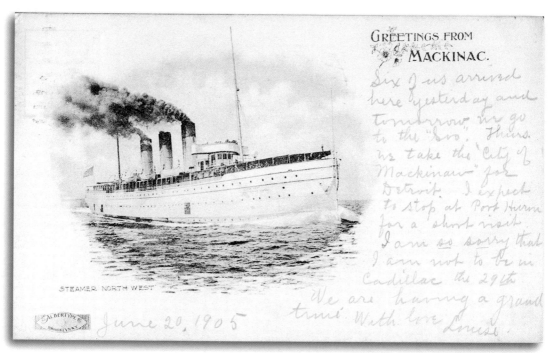

1. *The Albertype Co. issued a pre-1898 pioneer card of one of the steamers that frequented the island. This is a circa 1898 reissue of the pioneer card.*

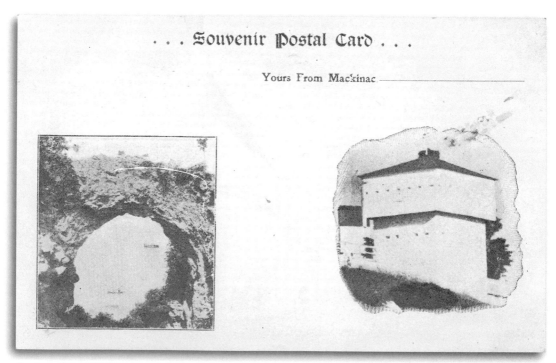

2. *Another 1898 reissue of a rare pioneer view card, this one with Arch Rock and Fort Mackinac's West Blockhouse. Both subjects became some of the most popular for post-cards in the next few years.*

3. This 1898 card is typical of turn-of-the-century graphic design and shows the high quality of German lithography. Though tiny, the images are remarkably detailed.

4. Another 1898 German multi-view by the same publisher.

MACKINAC FROM THE FORT.

5. *View of the village from the east end of Fort Mackinac. The Soldiers' Garden below the fort would be transformed into Marquette Park within the next decade (see 41 – 43).*

THE OLD FORT, MACKINAC ISLAND, MICHIGAN.

6160. COPYRIGHT, 1899, BY DETROIT PHOTOGRAPHIC CO.

6. *This early Detroit Publishing Co. view of Fort Mackinac gives a good view of the barns and other buildings located at the rear of the Soldiers' Garden.*

MACKINAC ISLAND FROM ROUND ISLAND, MICHIGAN.

5143. COPYRIGHT, 1899, BY DETROIT PHOTOGRAPHIC CO.

7. This Detroit Publishing Co. (note original name at bottom of card) panorama was also produced in a large, frameable print.

OLD MISSION
SOUVENIR POSTAL CARD
The Missionary Pioneer House of the Fairy Isle.
"EAST END,"   S. R. FRANKS, Propr.
Mackinac Island, Mich.,
190.

ARCH
ROCK

OLD
Mission—
—Church.

8. S. R. Franks, owner of the Mission House hotel, probably ordered this card for use by his guests. Note the blank space for the message at the center, rather than at the more typical side or bottom.

Porcelain plate by Luckybuck Studios, Germany.
Porcelain pitcher, Germany, both ca. 1905.

We drove about the island this morning. It is beautiful here now (am well now).
This P.M. we are going to see the unveiling of the monument to Fr. Marquette.
-Carrie, September 1, 1909

. . . This is some place; lots of people here now; very cold.
I am going fishing this morning.
-Herbert, August 23, 1913

Came to this Island this a.m. by speed boat and will return by
steamer. This weather is so cool and nice that our coats feel good.
-Florence Barr, August 13, 1935

Half the Fun:
Steamships
Docks &
Harbor Views

MACKINAC ISLAND.

Dear Daddy:—
Wishing you many
happy birthdays.
I remain your eldest daughter,
Laurel Squier.
July 5th/06.

9. *Mackinac Island was a premiere stop for Great Lakes passenger cruise lines. This early undivided back for the "Anchor Line" (Erie & Western Transportation Co.) features their three earlier vessels (1871) at the left (see also no. 21) along with the new* Tionesta *(1903).*

ARRIVAL OF STEAMSHIP TIONESTA AT DOCK, MACKINAC ISLAND, MICH.

10. *The Anchor Line was later acquired by the Pennsylvania Railroad. The* Tionesta *was one of three identical passenger sister ships named for locations in Pennsylvania. The others were the* Octorara *(1910) and* Juniata *(1905).*

ONE OF THE PALATIAL LAKE-LINERS OF THE GREAT LAKES TRANSIT CORP. FLEET.

11. The Octorara *under way. The Anchor Line vessels sailed between Buffalo and Detroit.*

S. S. North American
at Mackinac Island, Michigan

12. The North American *and* South American *were two of the last passenger ships to visit Mackinac Island. The* North *made her last visit in 1962 and the* South *in 1967.*

7 DECKS. COST $1,250,000. 6000 H. P. ENGINE. LENGTH, 444 FEET. BEAM 96.5 FEET.

12085 STR. "CITY OF CLEVELAND."   COPR. DETROIT PUBLISHING CO.

13. The Detroit & Cleveland Navigation Company's City of Cleveland III *was launched in 1907.*

STEAMSHIP "MANITOU," NORTHERN MICHIGAN TRANS. CO.

14. The fast sailing Manitou *made runs between Mackinac Island and Chicago in twenty-four hours and was relied upon for carrying fresh foods for island hotels and restaurants.*

Steamer "Islander".   MACKINAC ISLAND, Mich.

15. The Arnold Transit Co. carried railroad passengers from the mainland as well as offering daily excursions to the Les Cheneaux Islands. The wood-hulled Islander *was built in 1895 and last saw service in 1931.*

STEAMSHIP "MINNESOTA" CHICAGO-DULUTH TRANS. CO.

16. Originally built as the freighter Harlem *in 1888, this vessel was rebuilt as a passenger steamer in 1911 and renamed* Minnesota. *In 1915 she was chartered to the Michigan Transportation Co. to operate on weekly cruises between Chicago and Sault Ste. Marie.*

17. The view of the town and fort that still greets island visitors today.

18. The dock at right was used for passenger and freight traffic. To the left is the "coal dock," that still exists as a reminder of the days of steam.

OLD FORT AND PARK, MACKINAC ISLAND. MICH.

19. A tranquil view of Haldimand Bay, ca. 1905

7542. Mackinac Bay and City, Mackinac Island, Mich.

20. This view of the bay from Fort Mackinac dates to about 1910. The ship in the distance was likely added by the printer.

Mackinac Island, Mich.

240 Harbor View

21. *The Anchor Line's* India *at the dock with Arnold's* Islander *moored at the end.*

10019. THE DOCK AND MISSION POINT, MACKINAC ISLAND, MICH.

RAILROAD & STEAMBOAT
TICKET-OFFICE.

22. *View of Arnold's dock from Huron (Water) Street. By 1907, seven steamship lines made stops at the island.*

12106 ARNOLD'S DOCK, MACKINAC ISLAND, MICH.

23. *The dock crowded with travelers in about 1908. Most passenger vessels stopped for several hours, allowing visitors enough time to climb the hill to Fort Mackinac or take a carriage ride.*

Mackinac Island, Mich., Lake Front.

24. *These lads are likely showing off the catch from the commercial fishing boat behind them. Mackinac Island had been a center for such operations since the 1830s.*

25. *View of the east end of the village with a "Mackinaw Boat" in the foreground.*

26. *Small sailing craft, either for fishing like the* Silver Chief, *or pleasure, have been part of the island landscape for over two-hundred years.*

27. View from the east end of Haldimand Bay in about 1908.

28. Your water need not be liquid to go sailing. Ice boating was a popular winter pastime in many northern locations.

Porcelain plate (left) by Johnroth Studios, Germany for G. H. Wickman. Sterling spoon with enameled bowl, ca. 1900. Porcelain plate (below) by Wheelock, Germany for John Schwegler.

Was in this Church (Mission Church). Very old fashion; inside door to every seat.
-Richard, August 26, 1906

Am now on the job. There are about 40 Michigan fellows working on the island. Like it very much.
-B.J.B., July 2, 1915

Village Charm: Main Street, Churches & Cottages

Arnold's Dock, Mackinac Island, Mich.

29. *The entrance to the island from the Arnold Dock to Huron Street. Doud Brother's original grocery store (destroyed by fire in 1942) is to the left.*

MAIN STREET, MACKINAC ISLAND.

30. *View from the far west end of Huron Street in about 1901. Concrete sidewalks had made their appearance, but the street would not be paved until the 1920s. Other island streets and park roads were paved after World War II.*

31. With the Chippewa Hotel (left) the corner of Huron and Fort Streets has an almost metropolitan air. While it exudes Victorian charm, this street scene is much different than it had been a few decades earlier. Some island visitors at the time bemoaned this "modern progress" and loss of tranquility.

32. One of the most distinctive features on Huron Street from the 1870s until about 1950 was the tower atop the old Opera House. It was also remembered as "Fenton's Bazaar" from the souvenir store housed on the first floor. Photographer William Gardiner maintained his studio here (note the sign on the tower's top).

33. A view looking east along Huron Street from the corner of Astor Street in about 1905.

34. Compare this view with the one above. Note the different color selections made of the same location by the different publishers.

Main Street, Mackinac Island, Mich.

A1976

35. The views of Huron Street on these two pages would look familiar to any island visitor from the last 100 years. The look, scale and activities of the island's main street had solidified by the turn of the twentieth century and have changed little since.

MAIN STREET, MACKINAC ISLAND, MICH.

CARRIAGES LINED UP FOR STATE PARK DRIVE   NO AUTOS ALLOWED ON ISLAND

36. By 1925 the lack of autos on the island had become a novelty. They were banned by the village in 1898 and from the State Park three years later. Note also the utility poles (present since 1901) have been removed and street lights added.

37. *Not much has changed between the early part of the century and this mid-century view. Those intimately familiar with the island's history can pick out the empty spots where destruction and fire have removed a few structures (see 29 and 69).*

38. *The Opera House still has its tower in this circa 1940 shot. Bailey's Drug Store, founded by former Fort Mackinac post surgeon Dr. John Bailey, first opened in the 1880s. The little building was razed in 1997.*

39. A view from the East Bluff from about 1910.

40. The west end of the village with the Lakeview Hotel at lower right and Grand Hotel in the distance. French Lane is at the center.

41. *A view from Fort Mackinac of the east end of the village from about 1907. The Soldiers' Garden below the fort (see 93) is being transformed into Pere Marquette Place.*

42. *Mackinac National Park, created in 1875, was transferred to the State of Michigan in 1895. One of the first major projects of the Mackinac Island State Park Commission was the creation of an ornamental park to honor seventeenth-century explorer and missionary, Father Jacques Marquette.*

43. The park included curving paths, lawns and flower beds. It would eventually include the island's largest concentration of lilac trees. The annual Mackinac Island Lilac Festival was first held in 1948.

44. The centerpiece of the park was a bronze statue of Father Marquette erected through the efforts of Park Commissioner Peter White. Here visitors gather around the flag draped statue for the September 1, 1909 dedication.

A36—A SUMMER AFTERNOON IN MARQUETTE PARK, MACKINAC ISLAND, MICH.

45. Located within the island's business district, Marquette Park became a popular resting spot for weary tourists. The 1915 U. S. Coastguard Station can be seen in front of the Chippewa Hotel in the left distance. The station is now the Mackinac Island State Park Visitor's Center.

THE FORT AND MARQUETTE PARK, MACKINAC ISLAND, MICH.   54799

46. The park is dominated by Fort Mackinac. Although today it is popular for Frisbee and sun bathing, early visitors kept off the grass and were fully clothed.

47. *The Marquette Statue was made by Italian sculptor Gaetano Trentanove. It is a replica of his original marble statue in Statuary Hall in the U. S. Capitol. Another bronze version is in Marquette, Michigan.*

Old Fort Mackinac with Fr. Marquette Statue in Foreground, Mackinac Island, Mich.

48. *For a time during the mid-twentieth century "Old Fort Mackinac" was spelled with stones below the fort, as can be seen in both this image and the one above. Vandals occasionally had fun rearranging the letters.*

ST. ANN'S CHURCH, MACKINAC ISLAND, MICH.   96674

49. St. Anne's Catholic Church register dates to 1696; the parish traces its origin to the St. Ignace Mission. It was reestablished at Michilimackinac after 1714 and moved to Mackinac Island in 1781.

50. St. Anne's has occupied three buildings on two locations on Mackinac Island since the late 1700s. The current structure was built in 1873 and enlarged in the 1890s. It is an active parish today.

51. Rev. William Ferry established a Protestant mission on the island in 1823. It included a boarding school and in 1830 this church was constructed to house the growing Presbyterian congregation (see 112, 116 and 117).

52. Little Stone Church on Cadotte Avenue was completed in 1904 by members of the island's summer community.

7543. Young's Cottages and Road to the Fort, Mackinac Island, Mich.

53. *The Lawrence Young family of Chicago built this cottage on leased park land in 1902. Since 1945 it has been the Governor of Michigan's official summer residence. Was the out-of-scale auto added as a joke or did the printer think it was needed for visual interest?*

SUMMER HOME OF THE LATE
MICHAEL CUDAHY. MACKINAC ISLAND, MICH.

54. *"Stonecliffe" on the island's western shore was constructed in 1901. It was designed by the same architect as the Young Cottage above. The largest private cottage on the island, it is now a hotel.*

55. *Cottage construction on the East and West Bluffs (on land leased from the park), began in the 1880s.*

COTTAGES AND MARQUETTE PARK, MACKINAC ISLAND, MICH.

56. *The three cottages to the east of Marquette Park are also on leased state land. The George T. Arnold house on the far right, built by the Arnold Transit Company's founder, is one of the few constructed as a year-around residence.*

MACKINAC AND ROUND ISLAND, FROM WEST END.

57. A view from the West Bluff cottages circa 1900.

58. Many of the larger summer cottages were built in the 1890s and 1900s, replacing or incorporating more modest ones built just a few decades before.

59. A view from Pontiac's Lookout Trail looking east from the West Bluff about 1910.

60. This same view today has changed little, except for the Mackinac Bridge in the distance.

Stoneware cup with Grand Hotel, ca. 1895 and a variety of souvenirs from ca. 1930-1950 including a paperweight, pocket lighter, bullet pencil and bottle opener.

Madam, Opened July 1. Remember us to all friends coming north. This looks like Mackinac's banner year. Hope you will favor us with your presence too sometime during the season . . . Yours respectfully

-L. Metevier (of Lachance Cottage), July 7, 1915

It's 50 degrees here—some change . . . An ideal spot for both of you to visit.

-Love, Gertrude, July 22, 1947

TRAVELER'S REST: ISLAND HOTELS

Mackinac Island, Mich.

260 Island House

MANUFACTURED BY CURT TEICH & CO., CHICAGO, ILL.

61. Island House is the oldest hotel on Mackinac Island; its central section (seen here at right) dates to 1852.

ISLAND HOUSE AND EAST BLUFF, MACKINAC ISLAND, MICH.

62. The west wing (1895) and columned east wing (ca. 1900) were added to Island House in the late 1890s to accommodate growing numbers of tourists.

63. The Lakeview Hotel is located at the west end of Huron Street.

64. Originally built in 1858, the Lakeview Hotel was enlarged by the end of the century.

65. *The Chippewa Hotel was built in 1903. Arriving visitors were informed that it offered the European Plan (meals not included with the price of a room).*

66. *By 1910 an addition was added to the southeast corner of the building, adding several rooms and an expanded dining room.*

67. Originally built as a private residence in 1903, the Iroquois became a hotel in 1907 under the management of Samuel Poole, former state park superintendent.

68. Poole doubled the house in size with an extensive rear addition.

7527. New Mackinac and New Murray Hotels, Mackinac Island, Mich.

69. The New Mackinac replaced the earlier Mackinac House, destroyed by fire in 1887. In 1938 the vacant hotel was purchased by the city and torn down to create a park.

ST. CLOUD PLACE
MACKINAC ISLAND, MICH.

70. St. Cloud Place is located on the east end of the village. It no longer serves as a hotel, but as a dormitory for summer staff.

CHATEAU BEAUMONT, OVERLOOKING STRAITS OF MACKINAC

71. Chateau Beaumont on the east end of the village.

Lachance Cottage, Mackinac Island, Mich.

72. Lachance Cottage, next door to Chateau Beaumont above.

8847. GRAND HOTEL, MACKINAC ISLAND, MICH. COPYRIGHT, 1905, BY DETROIT PHOTOGRAPHIC CO.

Having a fine time. Rember me to gertude K. Yours as ever Karl.

73. *Built in 1887 by a conglomerate consisting of the Detroit & Cleveland Navigation Co. and two railroads, Grand Hotel ushered in a new era in tourism on Mackinac Island.*

9871 GRAND HOTEL. MACKINAC ISLAND, MICH. COPYRIGHT 1906 BY DETROIT PUBLISHING CO.

74. *The hotel dominates the approach to the island as only Fort Mackinac did before. The world's largest summer hotel, the sight of it has been one of the lasting impressions of a visit to the island for over a century.*

GRAND HOTEL   MACKINAC ISLAND MICH.   StL

75. The hotel weathered the depression without closing, unlike a number of its smaller competitors.

GRAND HOTEL BY MOONLIGHT–MACKINAC ISLAND, MICH.   3A-H1360

76. Actually, Grand Hotel in sunlight. The night and the moon, and probably the boats, were added by the printer.

THE GRAND HOTEL, MACKINAC ISLAND. MICH.

This doesn't look like our verandah does it.

77. *Originally the hotel was shorter, the east end stopping at the seventh column. In 1897 the east end was extended.*

GRAND HOTEL, MACKINAC ISLAND, MICH.

78. *The lower section beneath the porch was enclosed in the early part of the twentieth century.*

THE GRAND HOTEL, MACKINAC ISLAND, MICH.

79. In 1912 the top floor above the porch was greatly expanded. Minor physical changes, including a remodeled porte cochere and enclosed cupola were made in the 1980s.

GRAND HOTEL, MACKINAC ISLAND, MICH.
BELIEVE IT OR NOT   BY RIPLEY
LONGEST PORCH IN THE WORLD
Length 880 Feet

80. No one has disproved the longest porch claim since owner W. Stewart Woodfill convinced Mr. Ripley to feature it in his famous "Believe It Or Not" newspaper column in the 1930s. It is actually 628 feet long, however.

81. A view along the front of the porch from about 1910. In the 1970s and 80s major restoration was made to the porch columns, replacing the hollow centers with steel beams.

82. The exterior of the hotel changed little throughout the twentieth century. In 1998 and 2001 major expansions were made to the west and east ends of the building.

83. *While the exterior of the building retains its Victorian charm, the interior spaces have been redecorated numerous times to keep up with changing tastes. This is the Ball Room (or "Blue Room" as it was then known) as it appeared in 1938.*

84. *The Casino (meaning "club house," not gambling den) is now called the theatre. It had originally resembled a frontier opera house, but by 1938 could outdo the swankiest Hollywood nightclub.*

GRAND HOTEL SWIMMING POOL, MACKINAC ISLAND, MICH.

4791-29

85. Hotel managers sought the addition of a pool for many years and finally had one built in the 1920s.

Scene from the M.G.M. Motion Picture, "This Time for Keeps"

Grand Hotel Grounds, Mackinac Island, Michigan

7B-H500

86. Part of the story of M-G-M's 1947 musical This Time For Keeps *was set on Mackinac Island. A number of outdoor scenes were shot on the island, including several with Esther Williams in the pool. In 1987 the pool was renamed in her honor.*

GOLF LINKS, SHOWING OLD FORT IN DISTANCE, MACKINAC ISLAND, MICHIGAN.   103089

87. The Grand Hotel golf course was established to the east of the hotel in 1917. Part of the land, the former U. S. Army pasture, is leased from the state park.

GRAND HOTEL AND GROUNDS, MACKINAC ISLAND, MICH.

88. Golf of the miniature variety made a brief appearance at Grand Hotel as documented in this view, circa 1925.

Porcelain plate, Jonroth Studios,
England for G. H. Wickman, ca.
1910 and porcelain basket made in
Germany, ca. 1900.

*Am trying to add a little bright and bury my tired
nerves in this autoless island.*
-Aunt Nellie, August 14, 1920

Dear Baby, A long time ago they had soldiers here.
-Aunt Ellen, August 30, 1910

HISTORY'S
HOME

OLD FORT AND HARBOR, MACKINAC ISLAND, MICH.
5148. COPYRIGHT, 1899, BY DETROIT PHOTOGRAPHIC CO.

89. Fort Mackinac was one of the most popular postcard subjects, particularly views of the 1798 West Blockhouse.

Block House and Village, Mackinac Island, Mich.
PUB. BY G. H. WICKMAN.

90. The fort from the west had also been a popular stereoview image since the 1870s. Today, trees obscure this view.

Old Block House and Slopes, Mackinac Island, Mich.

PUBLISHED BY
J. H. SCHWEGLER.

91. Merchant J. H. Schwegler was possibly taking advantage of the new law allowing divided backs to prominently feature a little advertisement in the space previously used for the message.

92. Note how only the Schwegler card above has a flag pole emanating from the top of the blockhouse. The feature was added by the German printer.

Old Fort, Mackinac Island, Mich.

We are at St Ignace across from this Island for Bill's hay fever It is lonely Love to all. Laura H LaSue

93. *A view of the fort and the Fort Garden (see 5, 6, 41-43) circa 1902. The Perry Cannon is now exhibited within Fort Mackinac.*

OLD BLOCK HOUSE AND ROAD TO FORT. MACKINAC ISLAND. MICH.

94. *The fort approach and corner of the garden at the turn of the century.*

95. *Note the roofers on the top of the Guard House at the upper right. The little flag-draped platform is for the 1907 dedication of a plaque honoring fort commander Brigadier General Thomas Williams, killed at the Battle of Baton Rouge in 1862.*

Mackinac Island, Mich., Old Fort.

96. *View across the front of Officers' Stone Quarters. Begun by the British in 1780, it is one of the oldest buildings in Michigan. Many of the buildings inside Fort Mackinac were leased as summer cottages by the park after 1895, explaining the "not public" warning on the gate.*

97. After the U.S. took control of Fort Mackinac in 1796, three block houses were added. Here is the most photographed of the three (see 89-92) from within the fort.

98. The wooden palisades had disappeared from the fort walls by the middle of the 1800s. The army replaced them with rail and picket fences.

99. *The West Blockhouse was actually built in 1798. The palisades have returned in this 1940s view, restored by the Civilian Conservation Corp during the 1930s (see 146).*

100. *Fort Mackinac provides one of the best views on the island. Even the army commented on the tenacity of visitors, eager to make it up to the fort to take in the view.*

101. Wood Quarters (left) and Stone Quarters on the parade ground as they still appear every winter, with visitors gone and the Straits frozen.

102. A variety of functions took place within the fort in addition to a public pleasure ground and cottage rentals. Stone Quarters was designated as a museum in 1914 and the Old Post Hospital became the community "Beaumont Emergency Hospital" in 1923.

TEA ROOM, OFFICERS QUARTERS, FORT MACKINAC, MACKINAC ISLAND, MICH.

103. The Park Commission granted permission to open a tea room in the lower level of Stone Quarters in 1917 (originally run by the Red Cross). It operated on and off again over the next forty years and has been a continuous feature of Fort Mackinac since 1958.

Mackinac Island, Mich., Old Fort.

104. A view of the fort from the Army Pasture, now the Grand Hotel golf course (see 87).

Fort Holmes, Mackinac Island, Mich.

Climbed to the top 8/22/06 — girl fell from top + was killed this week —

GFA

PUB. BY G H. WICKMAN.

105. Built by the British following their 1812 capture of the island, Fort Holmes protected the heights behind Fort Mackinac. The first observation tower for tourists was built after the Civil War. This is the last and tallest one. Note the souvenir stand to the right.

OLD FORT ON HIGHEST POINT
OF MACKINAC ISLAND, MICH.

106. Legend was that one of the barns in the Fort Garden (see 5, 41) was constructed from the blockhouse at Fort Holmes (abandoned in the 1820s). When Marquette Park was created, the old barn was returned to the site. It later burned.

Fort Holmes, Mackinac Island, Mich.

107. A WPA crew reconstructed Fort Holmes in 1936 based on original army plans.

108. British Landing, the enemy's invasion point of 1812, was memorialized by the Park Commission with this monument in the early 1900s.

109. On the island's west shore, British Landing is a popular stop for those exploring the island's shoreline.

110. *This card from circa 1910 reproduced a view of the island from 40 years earlier. The U.S. Indian Agency Dormitory is seen at the center. This building later served as the island's public school from the 1870s until the middle 1960s.*

111. *The "House of Anne" was built as the Indian agent's residence. It was immortalized in Constance Fenimore Woolson's novels set on the island.*

112. Mission Church was the first building restored on Mackinac Island, completed through the efforts of interested summer residents in 1895. In 1955 the church was given to the Park Commission.

THE OLD FORT, LOOKING UP ASTOR STREET, MACKINAC ISLAND, MICH.
(OLDEST HOUSE ON ISLAND IN FOREGROUND)

113. Many of the early nineteenth-century buildings on Huron Street disappeared in the decades following the Civil War as the island developed into a major resort. Changes were less dramatic here on Market Street (not Astor Street), and turn-of-the-century visitors admired its rustic charm.

114. *The picturesque Biddle House. Market Street was not free from development. The older Mitchell House across the street had borne the "oldest house" title in numerous stereoviews a few decades earlier. It had since been torn down.*

115. *The Edward Biddle House was the last survivor of late eighteenth-century architecture on Market Street. It was carefully studied during the 1930s, restored by the Detroit Chapter of the American Institute of Architects in the 1950s and donated to the Park Commission.*

First Protestant Mission north of Detroit founded 1828.

116. Reverend Ferry's mission became the Mission House hotel in 1852. It served this purpose well into the twentieth century.

OLD MISSION, MACKINAC ISLAND, MICH.

117. The building survived the development of Mission Point into the headquarters of the Moral Re-Armament in the 1950s (now Mission Point Resort). It was acquired by the Park Commission in 1982.

118. *Like Mission House, the headquarters of the American Fur Company also were con-verted to housing travelers. Here, connected to form the John Jacob Astor House hotel, are the warehouse and the company agent's residence (Stuart House).*

119. *The east end of the hotel was the former company clerks' quarters. The warehouse (now the Community Center) and Stuart House (City Museum) were acquired by the city and restored. The Clerks' Quarters, however, was torn down in the middle 1950s.*

Custard cup, ca. 1910. Porcelain plate made in Germany for John B. Doud. Porcelain shoe, ca. 1905.

Up here with Uncle Harry. Don't miss this spot— wonderful and thrilling beyond words.

-Love, Sam, August 16, 1950

I have almost forgotten what hay fever is and am having a swell time. Wish you were here.

-Joe Gellis, Jr., September 10, 1933

Dear Letitia, Arrived here last evening and had a very pleasant trip. A little cool Sat. and Sun. but now the weather is just fine. This is the place for a rest. Mackinac has N.Y. beat. You had better take this trip next time. With love,

-Auna Unsweld, August 27, 1917

NATURE'S GRANDEUR

Authoress of "Anne"—The Mackinac Island Story

96676-N

120. "Anne's Tablet," a memorial to author Contance Fenimore Woolson, was erected in a small grove to the east of the fort in 1916.

IN THE WOODS, MACKINAC ISLAND, MICH.

121. The desire to turn Mackinac Island into a park in the 1870s was largely to insure the preservation of views such as these.

Copyright 1905 by the Rotograph Co.
G 7522 Drive, Mackinac Island, Mich.

122. When Mackinac National Park was transferred to Michigan in 1895 it encompassed 50% of the island. Today Mackinac Island State Park includes nearly 83%.

DWIGHTWOOD SPRING, EAST SHORE BOULEVARD
MACINAC ISLAND, MICH.

123. Edwin O. Wood donated this pergola over a natural spring in honor of his son Dwight who drowned in 1905. Wood was a Flint judge, Park Commissioner and author of a two volume history of Mackinac.

124. *Then as now a carriage tour was one of the most popular activities on the island. Business was very good at the turn of the century, and it was the carriage tour companies who had the most to gain from banning automobiles from the island.*

125. *Roads and trails curve throughout the island's interior as well as the shore. The shore road later became state highway M-185, the only highway in the state that forbids automobiles.*

9870. AN AUTUMN SCENE, MACKINAC ISLAND, MICH.

126. The serenity of the island's interior remains unchanged today.

12625 FAIRY ARCH, MACKINAC ISLAND, MICH.   COPR. DETROIT PUBLISHING CO.

127. The island's rock formations abound and are christened with a variety of descriptive or romantic names. They have been the subject of engravings, photographs and stereoviews as well as postcards. Alas, Fairy Arch was destroyed.

128. Arch Rock, the island's most popular natural wonder, not only to visit but also to commemorate with a postcard.

ARCH ROCK FROM LAKE, MACKINAC ISLAND.

129. From above and below the natural stone bridge has inspired sightseers and photographers.

Arch Rock, Mackinac Island, Mich.

130. *Many photographs have captured a view of a boat through the arch, which lends perspective to the shot. At least one of the boats in this view is probably real.*

ARCH ROCK, MACKINAC ISLAND. MICH.

131. *The sailboat in this view was added by the printer.*

132. There have been concerns over the arch's erosion since the 1850s. Portions of the top have been reinforced with concrete and visitors have long since been kept from climbing on top of the arch.

133. Note the visitors to the right. In the 1880s, before the age of postcards and personal cameras, the Foley Bros. would take your picture here. Dozens of photographs have survived showing groups of visitors atop the arch.

ARCH ROCK, FROM LAKE HURON, MACKINAC ISLAND, MICH.

134. The arch from the water before the road was built.

© ARCH ROCK, MACKINAC ISLAND, MICH.   3A-H1356

135. A mid-century view with an early viewing platform.

A 7523 Skull Cave, Mackinac Island, Mich.

136. In 1763 Alexander Henry was hidden here by his friend and protector, Wawatam. Henry reported that it was used as a sepulcher.

6163. GITCHIE MANITOU, MACKINAC ISLAND, MICH.   COPYRIGHT, 1902, BY DETROIT PHOTOGRAPHIC CO.

137. Along the eastern shore below Arch Rock prior to the road's construction.

138. Sugar Loaf, like Arch Rock, was a popular subject of engravings, photos and stereoviews.

139. The stairway, barely visible at the lower left of the rock, provided access to a small cave in the side.

AT ROBINSONS FOLLY, MACKINAC ISLAND.

140. A view of the newly constructed east shore road below Robinson's Folly.

COPR. DETROIT PUBLISHING CO.

71335 ROBINSON'S FOLLY, MACKINAC ISLAND, MICH. 127 FEET ABOVE THE LAKE

141. Robinson's Folly was celebrated in Victorian lore as the place where a love-sick soldier met his untimely end.

142. Lover's Leap on the western shore, as seen from the garden of the Weiss family cottage.

143. Of all the island landmarks, the waters of the Straits provide the most inspiration. This sunset view by Gardiner is from the west end of the village. The windmill was used to pump water from the lake.

12072

PINE POINT , WEST END BOULEVARD, MACKINAC ISLAND, MICH.

144. Another view by Gardiner captures both the water and the island's wooded charm.

145. Weary travelers exploring the island could find refreshment at the Cannon Ball located near British Landing.

146. The Civilian Conservation Corp camp near the 1814 Battlefield. The corps completed a number of projects on the island including restoration work at Fort Mackinac and construction of the park's Boy Scout Barracks in the 1930s.

Cup and saucer, Victoria, Carlsbad, Austria,
ca. 1900. Souvenir spoons often displayed several
island landmarks.

*...Am leaving here Wed. and get home Thursday. It has been one of the best
vacations I've ever had and feel so fat and fine. You had better try this place next
year. Save your pennies.*

-Estel, 1921

*Stopped off at Mackinac Island for an hour and a half this
afternoon and took a carriage to places of interest. It is a
wonderful place.*

-Hazel, July 2, 1922

The Mainland:
Mackinaw City,
The Straits Crossing
& St. Ignace

147. *Established in 1890 and completed three years later, Old Mackinac Point Light Station guided ships thought the Straits until 1957. "Old Mackinac Point" referred to the location of the 1714-1781 fort that had been moved to the island.*

STATE PARK AND AUTOMOBILE CAMP, MACKINAW CITY, MICH.   96677

148. *The light house was surrounded by a city park planned when the village was platted to preserve the location of Fort Michilimackinac. The park was given to the state in 1904 and placed under the care of the Mackinac Island State Park Commission in 1909.*

ENTRANCE TO STATE PARK, MACKINAW CITY, MICH.

5A-H2421

149. The Park Commission developed Michilimackinac State Park into a summer camp-ground in the 1910s and 1920s.

SCENE IN THE STATE PARK AT MACKINAW CITY MICH.

150. The Civil War era cannon was later turned over to the city. The concrete benches were designed by the park superintendent and many are still in use throughout Mackinac Island State Park.

151. The park included showers, a bandstand, a dance hall, a swimming dock and a small zoo. Camping at the park was ended in 1971.

152. In the 1930s the first reconstruction of the fort was completed. It included a palisade and several scattered buildings.

153. *There are those cannons again! The stone monument at the far right included a bronze plaque commemorating the attack of 1763 during Pontiac's Uprising.*

A-1441
SCENE AT OLD FORT MICHILIMACKINAC MACKINAW CITY, MICH.

154. *The museum and gift shop were a private concession.*

155. Wawatam Beach extends west of Michilimackinac State Park, where 170 cottages were constructed beginning in the early twentieth century. A walkway along the beach included two springs protected by rustic gazebos.

156. A view of the beach showing both the gazebos.

157. Like most "moonlight" postcards, this same view was also available in a "sunlight" version.

158. *Mackinaw City was first platted in 1857, but only developed after the arrival of the railroad in 1881.*

159. *Central Avenue, platted in 1857 as a grand boulevard, instead became a typical small-town main street with false-fronted storefronts.*

Main Street, Mackinaw City, Mich.

160. Mackinaw City had changed little by the 1940s.

STIMPSON
GOOSE MACKINAW CITY
MICH

161. The Stimpson House, here and left, offered the weary traveler a restful porch.

162. The village school was built in 1883 and expanded ten years later. The building was later sold, moved off-site and became a hotel.

NEW HIGH SCHOOL, MACKINAW CITY, MICH.   117992

163. Mackinaw City's new high school was built on the old site in 1927. It later served as the elementary school.

164. A wonderful example of depression-era stone work, the Mackinaw City Hall includes offices and the fire department.

165. As witnessed by the development of the campground at Michilimackinac State Park, the automobile brought a slow but steady change to the life of the sleepy village. Tourist cabins and other roadside amenities began to appear and came into their own in the post-war period.

Terminus of the Dixie Highway and East and West Michigan Pike, Mackinaw City, Mich.

166. This monument at the intersection of Central and Huron Avenues marked the terminus of the Dixie Highway, the Mackinaw Trail, the East Michigan Pike (running up the lower peninsulas east shore) and the West Michigan Pike (along the west shore).

167. Deer from the Upper Peninsula awaiting shipment by railroad to points south. By mid-century there were cars backed up for miles during hunting season and waits up to twelve hours to make the Straits of Mackinac crossing.

168. No ice shanty, but a tarp protected these anglers from the Straits bitter winds.

169. The railroad brought Mackinaw City into existence in the 1880s. Tourists embarked from here to island ferries or would continue their journey via railroad car ferry to St. Ignace.

170. The first railroad cars were towed on the scow "Betsy" by the early ice breaker Algomah *in the early 1880s. By the 1890s the railroad ferries carried an average of 300 to 350 railroad cars a day across the Straits.*

STATE AUTO FERRY AND DOCK, MACKINAW CITY, MICH.   109088

171. By the 1920s automobile ferries had joined the rail ferries.

Mackinaw City, Mich.

172. The improved state automobile ferry dock with Mackinaw City in the distance.

Steamer Chief Wawatam, Straits of Mackinac, Mich.

24409

173. The mighty **Chief Wawatam** *railroad car ferry plied the Straits between Mackinaw City and St. Ignace from 1911 until 1981. Operated by the Mackinac Transportation Company, the steam vessel could carry 26 railroad cars.*

174. Passengers rode up top in the cabins or enjoyed the view from the upper decks.

5496. STR. "SAINTE MARIE." STRAITS OF MACKINAW   PLIES BETWEEN ST. IGNACE AND MACKINAW CITY.

175. Chief Wawatam *was predated by the 1893 wood and steel-plated* Sainte Marie. *In 1913 the engines from the old* Sainte Marie *were used in a new steel-hulled vessel with the same name, built along the same lines as the* Chief.

CAR FERRIES, CHIEF WAWATAM AND ST. MARIE II STUCK IN THE ICE.

176. In addition to transporting railroad cars, the sister ships Chief Wawatam *and* Sainte Marie *were also ice breakers. They were often hired out to open shipping lanes at the Straits and through the St. Mary's River. The Department of Transportation also leased the vessels in the winter to transport automobiles when the regular car ferries were laid up.*

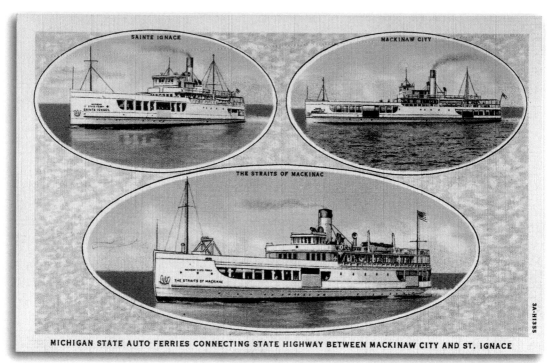

177. *With no bridge at the Straits and increased automobile traffic, the State Highway Department needed a means to connect the two peninsulas. The Michigan State Ferries were created by legislative act in 1923.*

178. *The* City of Munising *was built in 1904 as the railroad ferry* Pere Marquette No. 20 *running out of Ludington. She was purchased by the state and reconditioned, joining the Mackinac fleet in 1938.*

179. Added to the Straits of Mackinac fleet in 1937, the City of Cheboygan *was originally the* Ann Arbor IV *of the Ann Arbor Railroad Co. built in 1906 and used for years between Manitowoc and Frankfort.*

180. The 360 foot Vacationland *was an ice breaker ferry, added to the fleet in 1951. It could carry 150 cars and was one of the most powerful ships on the Great Lakes. Some felt that it would be able to take care of increased traffic and that a bridge across the Straits would not be necessary.*

New State Auto Ferry Dock, St. Ignace, Mich.

9A-H1731

181. The ferry dock in St. Ignace in 1939. In 1950 a larger dock was built to the south of town to accommodate the increased traffic.

State Auto Ferry Dock, St. Ignace, Mich.

7A-H3599

182. Another 1930s view of the St. Ignace dock. Arnold Transit Company's ferries to the island now embark from this point.

183. St. Ignace postcards promoted its rustic charm.

184. Graham's Point located on the south end of St. Ignace.

10026. ST. ANTHONY'S ROCK, ST. IGNACE, MICH.

COPYRIGHT 1906 BY DETROIT PUBLISHING CO.

185. Mackinac Island did not have a monopoly on scenic rocks. St. Anthony's Rock was located in the heart of the village of St. Ignace.

CASTLE ROCK, ST. IGNACE, MICH.

186. Just outside of St. Ignace is Castle Rock, located on private property.

CASTLE ROCK, ST. IGNACE,

187. By the 1930s a stairway led up the promontory to a lookout platform. A gift shop and parking lot were nestled below.

MARQUETTE PARK AND MONUMENT, ST. IGNACE, MICH.

188. Father Marquette founded a mission at St. Igance in 1671. His gravesite (now disputed) was located in the 1870s and this monument erected over the spot.

"La Salle High School". St. Ignace, Mich. 6/2-9-08.

Dear Friend -: myrtle is chasing a half breed down the street now. an indian just like herself. J. C.

No. 1932   Pub. in Germany for Mulcrone's Bazaar, St. Ignace, Mich.

189. LaSalle High School served the community for many years.

ST. IGNACE, MICHIGAN, SHOWING MACKINAC ISLAND IN THE DISTANCE   87769

190. A bird's eye view from about 1921. Modern St. Ignace is built upon the site of the 1671 mission of the same name. Fort de Buade was established nearby. Both were abandoned by the early 1700s.

NORTHERN MICHIGAN'S BIG ATTRACTION, INDIAN VILLAGE, ST. IGNACE, MICH.

COPYRIGHT 1931 BY C. C. EBY, ST. IGNACE, MICH.

191. St. Ignace's main street along Moran Bay. Indian Village was a popular tourist spot.

City of St. Ignace, Mich.

7A-H3603

192. The state auto ferry docks are visible in this mid-century view of the town.

St. Ignace and Straits of Mackinac, Mich.

193. View of the village from the late 1930s. The modern town dates to the middle 1800s. It was incorporated as a city in 1883.

APPENDIX:
PUBLISHER INFORMATION
& DATES OF THE CARDS

The following list includes the publisher ("np" means no publisher is indicated), any publication numbers, the date of publication and if the card was postmarked ("pm") followed by the postmark date.

Front Cover:
    Left: Detroit Publishing Co. 12069, 1908, pm Mackinac Island, 1908 (see number 92)
    Right: np, ca. 1910 (see number 130)
    Bottom: Detroit Publishing Co. 9871, 1906 (later reissue with divided back) (see number 74)

Page i: G. W. Wickman, ca. 1908, pm Wooster, Ohio, 1909.

Page ii: G. W. Wickman [Curt Teich?] A-9601, ca. 1908

Page v: Detroit Publishing Co. for W. H. Gardiner 12559, ca. 1908

Page vii: Curt Teich for G. W. Wickman OA4504-N, 1930

Page 1: Curt Teich for Benjamin's Photo Art Service 5A-H657 [reissue of an earlier Wickman view], ca. 1955 (1935)

Page 5: Curt Teich for G. H. Wickman 72604, 1917, pm Chicago, 1934

Page 6: Curt Teich for G. H. Wickman 5A-H718, 1935, pm Mackinac Island, 1948

Page 10 top: Curt Teich for Benjamin's Photo Art Service [reissue of earlier Wickman], ca. 1950.

Page 10 bottom: Detroit Publishing Co. 8852, 1905

Page 127: Detroit Publishing Co. 10120, ca. 1906, pm Mackinac Island, 1907

Page 137: Detroit Publishing Co. 6522, 1902, pm Mackinac Island, 1905

Page 140: G. W. Wickman, 1906, pm Mackinac Island, 1906

Back Cover: Detroit Publishing Co. 70595, ca. 1912, pm Mackinac Island, 1912

THE CARDS

1. Albertype Co. (pioneer view), pre-1898, pm Mackinac Island, 1905

2. n.p. (pioneer view) pre-1898 (post 1898 printing, ca. 1900)

3. Emil Pinkau & G. Leipzig (Germany), ca. 1898, pm Mackinac Island, 1900

4. Emil Pinkau & G. Leipzig (Germany), ca. 1898, pm Mackinac Island, 1901

5. E.C. Kropp, photo by H. J. Rossiter, ca. 1898

6. Detroit Publishing Co. 6160, 1899

7. Detroit Publishing Co. 5143, 1899

8. np, ca. 1900

9. np, ca. 1898, pm Buffalo, 1905

10. V. O. Hammon Publishing Co. 1247, ca. 1910

11. Detroit Publishing Co. 81906, ca. 1920, pm Mackinac Island, 1934

12. Curt Teich 2C-H1674 for Benjamin's, 1952

13. Detroit Publishing Co. 12085, 1908-09

14. V. O. Hammon, ca. 1910

15. The Albertype Co. for L. E. Edwards, ca. 1910

16. V. O. Hammon 1873, ca. 1915

17. Detroit Publishing Co. 1146, 1905

18. V. O. Hammon 1213, ca. 1905

19. L. E. Edwards (by a German printer), ca. 1905

20. np 7542, ca. 1915

21. Curt Teich, ca. 1905

22. Detroit Publishing Co. 10019, 1906

23. Detroit Publishing Co. 12106, 1908-09

24. The Hugh C. Leighton Co. 4932, ca. 1905

25. Detroit Publishing Co. 12073, 1908-09

26. Detroit Publishing Co. 9875, 1906

27. Hugh C. Leighton Co. 4946, ca. 1908

28. G. H. Wickman (by a German printer), ca. 1905

29. G. H. W. [Wickman] A7113 [Curt Teich?], ca. 1905

30. E. C. Kropp 1429, ca. 1898

31. Detroit Publishing Co. 8848, 1905

32. Hugh C. Leighton Co. 4945, ca. 1900

33. V. O. Hammon 1588, ca. 1905

34. Detroit Publishing Co. 12076, 1908-09

35. G.H.W. [Wickman], ca. 1905

36. E. C. Kropp for Frank Shama, ca. 1925

37. L. L. Cook Co. L-1619, ca. 1945

38. np, ca. 1940

39. G. H. Wickman, ca. 1910

40. G. H. Wickman A7109 [Curt Teich?], 1910

41. V. O. Hammon 1212, ca. 1905, pm Cheboygan, 1910

42. L. E. Edwards (by a German printer) 14, ca. 1905, pm Mackinac Island, 1909

43. V. O. Hammon 1211, ca. 1908, pm Mackinac, 1910

44. V. O. Hammon, 1909

45. V. O. Hammon A36, ca. 1915

46. Curt Teich for G. H. Wickman 54799, 1914, pm Mackinac Island, 1927

47. L. L. Cook Co. A-755, ca. 1945

48. Curt Teich for G. H. Wickman 1B-H1006, ca. 1940

49. Curt Teich for G. H. Wickman 96674, ca. 1923

50. The Rotograph Co. D 7525, 1905

51. Detroit Publishing Co. 6162, 1902

52. Curt Teich for G. H. Wickman 102826, ca. 1925

53. np, ca. 1910

54. V. O. Hammon 2158, ca. 1910

55. L. E. Edwards, ca. 1910, pm Mackinac Island, 1912

56. G. W. H. [Wickman] A-7117 [Curt Teich?], ca. 1910

57. E. C. Kropp 309, photo by H. J. Rossiter, ca. 1900, pm Mackinac Island, 1906

58. Detroit Publishing Co. 12050, 1908-09

59. The Albertype Co., published by Stewart & Preston, ca. 1910

60. For L. E. Edwards (by a German printer), ca. 1910

61. Curt Teich 260, ca. 1908, pm Mackinac Island, 1909

62. V. O. Hammon 1530, ca. 1910

63. E. C. Kropp 1436, ca. 1902-1907, pm Mackinac Island, 1907

64. L. E. Edwards 41, ca. 1910

65. The Rotograph Co. 7519b, ca. 1907

66. V. O. Hammon 1246, ca. 1910, pm 1911

67. V. O. Hammon 1564, ca. 1910

68. V. O. Hammon, ca. 1915

69. np, ca. 1910, pm Terre Haute, Indiana, 1911

70. V. O. Hammon, ca. 1910, pm Mackinac Island, 1923 [?]

71. The Albertype Co., ca. 1910

72. np [Rosenfield & Goodman?] "Octochrome," ca. 1915, pm Mackinac Island, 1915

73. Detroit Publishing Co. 8847, 1905, pm Mackinac Island, 1905

74. Detroit Publishing Co. 9871, 1906 (later reissue with divided back)

75. np (heavily retouched real photo card), ca. 1935

76. Curt Teich for G. H. Wickman 3A-H1360, 1931, pm Munising, Michigan, 1949

77. For L. E. Edwards (German), ca. 1905, pm Mackinac Island, 1910

78. [Curt Teich] for G. H. W. [Wickman] R-72602, ca. 1910

79. Curt Teich for G. H. W. [Wickman] R-86247, ca. 1915

80. E. C. Kropp for Frank Shama 31714, ca. 1935

81. V. O. Hammon 1273, ca. 1910

82. G. H. Wickman R-61018 [Curt Teich?], 1914

83. Curt Teich 8A-H264, 1938

84. Curt Teich 8A-H263, 1938

85. Curt Teich for G. H. Wickman 4791-29, 1929

86. Curt Teich for G. H. Wickman 7B-H500, 1947

87. Curt Teich for G. H. Wickman 109089, ca. 1926

88. np (2825IN) for John H. Schwegler, ca. 1925

89. Detroit Publishing Co. 5148, 1899

90. G. H. Wickman, ca. 1906, pm Mackinac Island, 1906

91. J. H. Schwegler (German), ca. 1908

92. Detroit Publishing Co. 12069, 1908, pm Mackinac Island, 1908

93. Curt Teich 230/54335, ca. 1902, pm St. Ignace, 1906

94. L. E. Edwards (German), ca. 1905

95. Detroit Publishing Co. 12071, 1908-09, pm Mackinac Island, 1917

96. The Hugh C. Leighton Co. 4939, ca. 1905

97. V. O. Hammon. ca. 1910

98. J. R. Johnson of Cheboygan (real photo card), ca. 1915

99. L. L. Cook Co. L-1622 (real photo card), ca. 1945, pm St. Ignace, 1949

100. Detroit Publishing Co. for W. H. Gardiner, 12074, 1908-09

101. Curt Teich for C. McKeever, The Studio D-8104, ca. 1950

102. V. O. Hammon, ca. 1925

103. V. O. Hammon, ca. 1930

104. The Hugh C. Leighton Co. 4930, ca. 1905

105. G. H. Wickman, ca. 1905, pm Petoskey, 1906

106. V. O. Hammon 2157, ca. 1910

107. E. C. K. [E. C. Kropp] (real photo card), ca. 1940

108. G. H. W. [Wickman], ca. 1908

109. E. C. Kropp 1439, ca. 1905

110. V. O. Hammon 1583, ca. 1910 (from an 1871 photo)

111. The Albertype Co. for John S. Doud, ca. 1910 (from ca. 1885 photo)

112. np, ca. 1910

113. V. O. Hammon 1245, ca. 1910

114. V. O. Hammon 1585, ca. 1910

115. G. W. Wickman (German), ca. 1908, pm Wooster, Ohio, 1909

116. Detroit Publishing Co. 6521, 1902

117. V. O. Hammon 1214, ca. 1910

118. V. O. Hammon 1205, ca. 1910

119. The Albertype Co., ca. 1910

120. Curt Teich for G. H. Wickman 96676-N, 1923

121. The Rotograph Co. E7525a, ca. 1910

122. The Rotograph Co. G-7522, 1905

123. V. O. Hammon 1565, ca. 1910

124. The Hugh C. Leighton Co. 4938, ca. 1905

125. np [Curt Teich?] A1378, ca. 1908-10, pm Mackinac Island, 1922

126. Detroit Publishing Co. 9870, ca. 1905-06 (reissue with divided back), pm Mackinac Island, 1914

127. Detroit Publishing Co. 12625, 1908-09

128. V. O. Hammon Publishing Co. 1210, ca. 1905 (reissue with divided back), pm Sault Ste. Marie, 1910

129. E. C. Kropp 1440, ca. 1905

130. np, ca. 1910

131. L. E. Edwards (German), ca. 1910

132. Detroit Publishing Co. 5147, 1899

133. Curt Teich 229, ca. 1905 (reissue with divided back)

134. The Albertype Co., ca. 1910, pm Mackinac Island, 1922

135. Curt Teich for G. H. Wickman 3A-H1356, 1933

136. The Rotograph Co. A-7523, 1905

137. Detroit Publishing Co. 6163, 1902

138. E. C. Kropp 310, photo by H. J. Rossiter, ca. 1900

139. Curt Teich 227, ca. 1905 (reissue with divided back), pm Detroit

140. E. C. Kropp 1443, ca. 1905

141. Detroit Publishing Co. for W. H. Gardiner 71335, 1913-18

142. np 7534, ca. 1910

143. Detroit Publishing Co. for W. H. Gardiner 9849, ca. 1910

144. Detroit Publishing Co. for W. H. Gardiner 12072, 1908-09

145. The Albertype Co., ca. 1910

146. np (real photo card), ca. 1935

147. Crescent Photo Co. (real photo card), ca. 1930

148. Curt Teich for G. H. Wickman 96677, 1923

149. Curt Teich for G. H. Wickman 5A-H2421, 1935

150. np (real photo card), ca. 1915

151. np (real photo card), ca. 1945

152. L . L. Cook A-1432 (real photo card), ca. 1940

153. Curt Teich for Mrs. C. C. Graham, Petoskey, Mich. 169, ca. 1940

154. L. L. Cook A-1441 (real photo card), ca. 1940

155. np (real photo card), ca. 1910, pm Mackinaw, 1911

156. Charles J. Herbert (real photo card), ca. 1940 *beach*

157. Curt Teich for G. H. Wickman 91208-N, ca. 1921 *cottage*

158. J. S. Desy, ca. 1910, pm Grand Rapids, 1910 *village*

159. np, ca. 1910

160. Curt Teich for G. W. Wickman 8B-H1581, 1941, pm [Michigan], 1955

161. np, ca. 1910, stamped but no pm; message dated 1912

162. np, ca. 1910, pm Rudyard, 1912 *high school*

163. Curt Teich for G. W. Wickman 117992, 1927

164. E. C. Kropp. [E. C. Kropp] (real photo card), ca. 1945

165. L. L. Cook (real photo card), ca. 1945

166. For J. H. Coffman & Son, ca. 1920

167. V. O. Hammon 1281, photo by Clyde Johnson, ca. 1915

168. For J. H. Coffman & Son, ca. 1920

169. V. O. Hammon 1282, ca. 1910

170. V. O. Hammon, photo by Clyde Johnson, Saginaw, ca. 1910, pm Chicago, 1918

171. Curt Teich for G. H. Wickman, 109088, 1926

172. np (real photo card), ca. 1945

173. Curt Teich for G. H. Wickman 24409, ca. 1911

174. Clyde Johnson, Mackinaw City, 1914, pm Grayling, 1914

175. Detroit Publishing Co. 5496, 1900 (reissue with divided back), pm Sault Ste. Marie, 1908

176. Curt Teich for G. H. Wickman (Copyright by J. S. Desy) R-3905, 1913

177. Curt Teich for G. H. Wickman 3A-H1355, 1933

178. np (real photo card), ca. 1945

179. E. C. K. (E. C. Kropp), ca. 1945

180. Curt Teich for C. C. Eby, St. Ignace 1C-P1999, 1951

181. Curt Teich for G. H. Wickman 9A-H1731, 1939, pm St. Ignace, 1944

182. Curt Teich for G. H. Wickman 7A-H3599, 1937

183. np, 4805, ca. 1907, pm Petoskey, 1910

184. [Curt Teich] for G. W. Wickman, (from postcard folder), 1926

185. Detroit Publishing Co. 10026, 1906, pm [illegible]

186. [Curt Teich] for G. W. Wickman, (from postcard folder), 1926

187. [Curt Teich] for G. W. Wickman, (from postcard folder), 1938

188. [Curt Teich] for G. W. Wickman, (from postcard folder), 1926

189. For Mulcrone's Bazaar (German), No. 1932, ca. 1900

190. Curt Teich for G. W. Wickman 87769, ca. 1921

191. E. C. Kropp for C. C. Eby, St. Ignace 10172, 1931

192. Curt Teich for G. W. Wickman 7A-H3603, 1937

193. Curt Teich for Wickman's Photo Shop, ca. 1950

BIBLIOGRAPHY

POSTCARDS AND SOUVENIRS

Burdick, J. R. *Pioneer Post Cards: The Story of Mailing Cards to 1898.* J. R. Burdick, 1957.

Burgess, Arene. *A Collector's Guide to Souvenir Plates.* Atglen, Pennsylvania: Schiffer Publishing, 1996.

Carline, Richard. *Pictures in the Post: The Story of the Picture Postcard.* Bedford, England: Gordon Fraser, 1959.

Curt Teich Postcard Archives, Lake County Museum, Wauconda, Illinois. Material consulted includes: Mackinac Island and Mackinaw City Geographic Indices and "Guide to Dating Curt Teich Postcards."

Hamilton-Smith, Catherine. "Postcards: The Pan-Document of the 20th Century." *Cultural Resources Management* 16:6 (1993): 16-17.

Morgan, Hal and Andreas Brown. *Prairie Fires and Paper Moons: The American Photographic Postcard: 1900-1920.* Boston: David R. Godine, 1981.

Rainwater, Dorothy T. and Donna H. Felger. *American Spoons: Souvenir and Historical.* Hanover, Pennsylvania: Everybodys Press, Inc., 1977.

Ryan, Dorothy B. *Picture Postcards in the United States, 1893-1918.* New York: Clarkson N. Potter, Inc., 1982.

Staff, Frank. *The Picture Postcard & Its Origins.* New York: Frederick A. Praeger, Publishers, 1966.

Stechschulte, Nancy Stickels. *The Detroit Publishing Company Postcards.* Big Rapids, Michigan: Nancy Stickels Stechschulte, 1994.

Williams, Laurence W. *Collector's Guide to Souvenir China: Keepsakes of a Golden Era.* Paducah, Kentucky: Collector Books, 1998.

Willoughby, Martin. *A History of Postcards.* New Jersey: Wellfleet Press, 1992.

Zaid, Barry. *Wish You Were Here: A Tour of America's Great Hotels During the Golden Age of the Picture Post Card.* New York: Crown Publishers, Inc., 1990.

STRAITS OF MACKINAC HISTORY

Armour, David A. *100 Years at Mackinac*: Mackinac Island, Mackinac State Historic Parks, 1995.

Calache , Lisa Dziabis. "William Henry Gardiner (1861-1935); An Early Canadian/American Photographer," *Photographic Canadiana* (September – October 1998): 8-13.

Lang, Otto W. "The Reminiscences of Otto W. Lang," 1975 (unpublished oral memoir transcribed by Mackinac Island State Park Commission). Mackinac State Historic Parks Library.

McKee, Russell. *Mackinac: The Gathering Place*. Lansing: Michigan Natural Resources Magazine, 1981.

Michigan gazetters *(Michigan State Gazetteer and Business Directory, Michigan Gazeteer, R. L. Polk and Company's Michigan Gazetteer)*, selected volumes, 1873-1932.

Petersen, Eugene T. *Mackinac Island: Its History In Pictures*. Mackinac Island: Mackinac Island State Park Commission, 1973.

Porter, Phil. *Mackinac: An Island Famous in These Regions*. Mackinac Island: Mackinac State Historic Parks, 1998.

_____. *View From The Veranda: The History and Architecture of the Summer Cottages On Mackinac Island*. "Reports in Mackinac History and Archaeology Number 8. Mackinac Island: Mackinac Island State Park Commission, 1981.

Ranville, Judy and Nancy Campbell. *Memories of Mackinaw*. Mackinaw City: Mackinaw City Public Library/Mackinaw City Woman's Club, 1976.

Wood, Edwin O. *Historic Mackinac: The Historical, Picturesque and Legendary Features of the Mackinac Country*. New York: The Macmillan Company, 1918.

ACKNOWLEDGMENTS

I express my thanks to the MSHP publications team: Chairperson Lynn Evans, Dave Armour, Ron Crandell, Carl Nold, Phil Porter and Tim Putman. I also wish to acknowledge the assistance of Debra Gust of the Lake County Discovery Museum in Wauconda, Illinois which preserves the Curt Teich Archives.

The Mackinac State Historic Parks postcard collection contains hundreds of individual cards collected over the past 40 years. A major collections effort launched in the middle 1990s increased our holdings significantly. This includes older cards as well as those from recent decades that do not appear in the book. I want to thank MSHP's former collections registrar Linnea Aukee Nurmi for her assistance during this major collections push.

Most of the cards in the collection have been gathered one or two at a time, usually from postcard dealers and other private sellers. We have over the years received numerous donations of postcards as well. We wish to acknowledge two donors whose gifts added greatly to the collection: Alicia Poole and Ken Neyer. The Poole Collection laid the foundation for the card collection in the 1960s and Mr. Neyer's donation in 1996 filled in many gaps.

INDEX

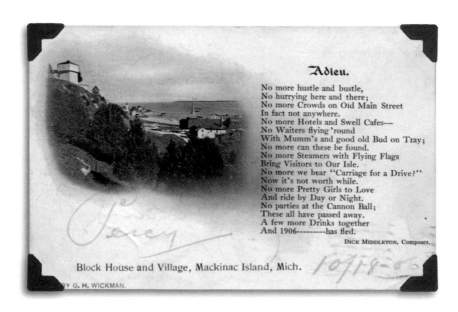

Adieu.

No more hustle and bustle,
No hurrying here and there;
No more Crowds on Old Main Street
In fact not anywhere.
No more Hotels and Swell Cafes——
No Waiters flying 'round
With Mumm's and good old Bud on Tray;
No more can these be found.
No more Steamers with Flying Flags
Bring Visitors to Our Isle.
No more we hear "Carriage for a Drive?"
Now it's not worth while.
No more Pretty Girls to Love
And ride by Day or Night.
No parties at the Cannon Ball;
These all have passed away.
A few more Drinks together
And 1906————has fled.

DICK MIDDLETON, Composer.

Block House and Village, Mackinac Island, Mich.

BY G. H. WICKMAN.

About the Author

Asixth-generation native of Michigan's Upper Peninsula, Steven Brisson grew up in western Alger County. He received a B.A. in History from Northern Michigan University in 1989 and a M.A. from the Cooperstown Graduate Program in History Museum Studies in 1992. His museum career began as a student assistant with the Michigan Bureau of History at the Michigan Iron Industry Museum and Fayette Historic Townsite. He completed a senior internship at the Henry Ford Museum & Greenfield Village in 1991. He served as a curator for the State Historical Society of Wisconsin Sites Division from 1992 through 1995. He became Curator of Collections for Mackinac State Historic Parks in 1996. He lives with his wife Lisa Craig Brisson, daughter Emma and son Matthew in Cheboygan.